SCIENCE THROUGH COOKERY

Hot and Cold

Peter Mellett
Jane Rossiter

FRANKLIN WATTS
London • New York • Sydney • Toronto

Franklin Watts
96 Leonard Street
London EC2A 4RH

Franklin Watts
14 Mars Road
Lane Cove
NSW 2066

UK ISBN: 0 7496 0927 3

10 9 8 7 6 5 4 3 2 1

Senior editor: Hazel Poole
Series editor: Jane Walker
Designer: Ann Samuel
Illustrator: Annabel Milne
Photographer: Michael Stannard
Consultant: Margaret Whalley

Additional photograph: p12, Simon Fraser/Science Photo Library

The publisher would like to thank the following children for their participation in the photography of this book: Tom Brownrigg, Caroline Rossiter, Alexander Rossiter and Corinne Smith-Williams.

A CIP catalogue record for this book is available from the British Library

Typeset by Spectrum, London
Printed in Singapore

Contents

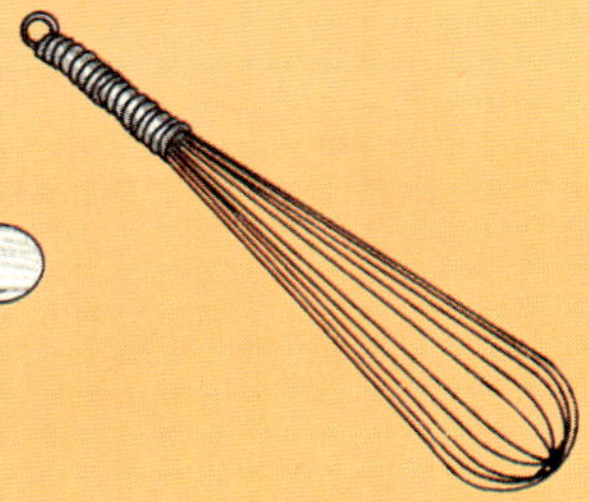

Introduction

Science Through Cookery is a new, simple and fun approach to learning about science. In each book you will not only read about science, but you will also have first-hand experience of real science. By linking science topics with simple cookery recipes, you can learn about science and at the same time cook some delicious recipes. Science is fun when you finish up eating the results of your work!

About this book

In **Hot and Cold,** we look at the topic of heat energy, and its effects on different substances. **Hot and Cold** explains temperature and how it is measured, and investigates the various ways that heat can move from one place, or object, to another.

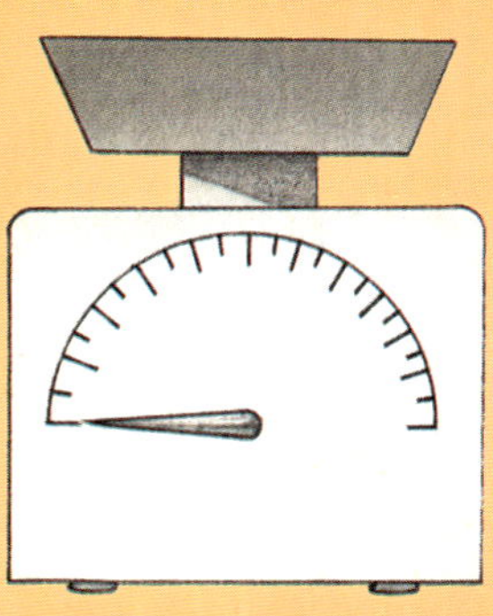

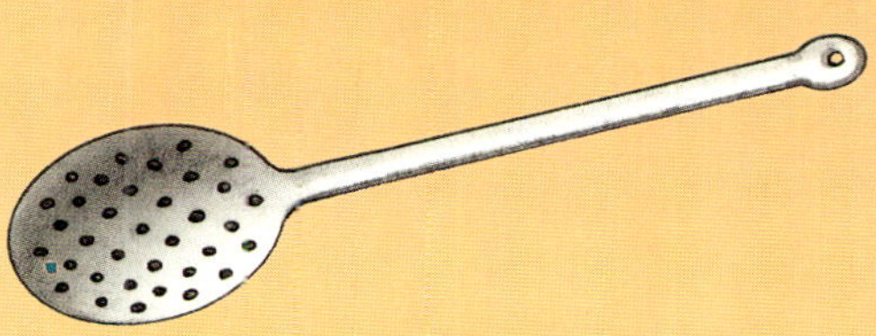

Hot and Cold explains important scientific principles with the help of clearly labelled diagrams and illustrations. The recipes offer a practical opportunity to gain a better understanding of the science you have just read about.

Each recipe has been carefully selected and written so that the cookery can be done by children with a minimum amount of adult supervision. Where the help of an adult is needed, for example when boiling a pan of water, this is clearly indicated.

The ingredients and equipment you will need are listed at the beginning of each recipe. They are easily obtainable and no specialist equipment is required. The step-by-step format of the recipes is easy to follow. Each step is illustrated with a photograph.

At the end of the book you will find a page of Further things to do. These are fun experiments and activities which are linked to many of the science concepts discussed in the book. A glossary of terms and an index are provided at the end of the book.

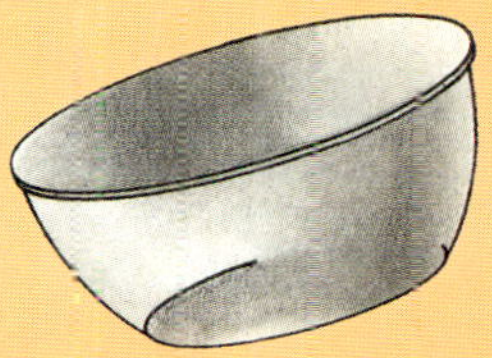
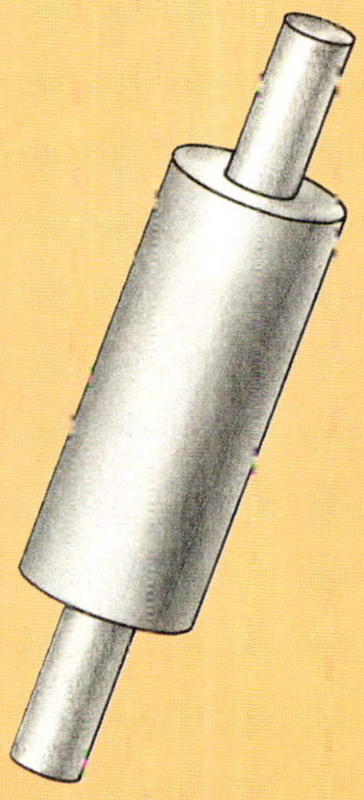

Solid, liquid or gas?

Everything in the world is either a solid, a liquid or a gas. Solid substances are firm and do not change their shape. Liquids are runny and can be poured from one container to another. Gases are usually invisible and spread out to fill the space around them.

Every solid, liquid and gas is made up from tiny invisible pieces called atoms. In most substances, the atoms are joined together in separate groups called molecules.

Ice lollies

<u>Ingredients</u>
500 ml pure fruit juice, such as orange, pineapple or apple juice

Equipment

a measuring jug
a tablespoon
8 ice lolly moulds
8 wooden sticks
a plastic container

1 Check with an adult how to switch the freezer, or the ice box of the fridge, to its coldest setting. Place a stick in each lolly mould.

2 Carefully pour the fruit juice into the jug and stir it well. Pour the juice into the moulds, and put them in the freezer or ice box.

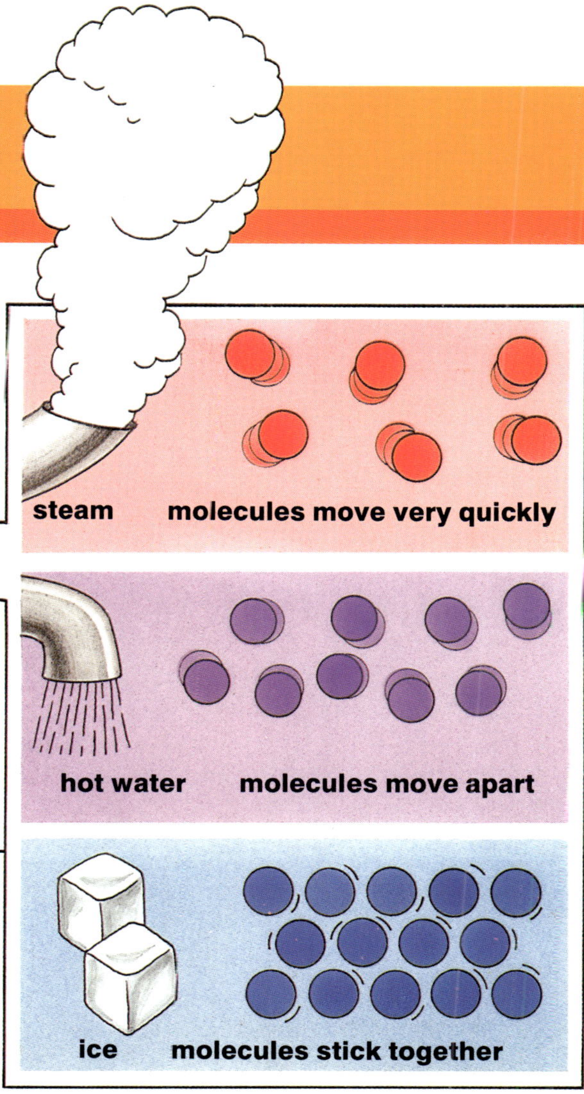

Water is made from molecules that are all the same. The molecules in liquid water move about freely all the time. When water is heated, the molecules in it move faster. The hotter the water, the quicker the molecules move. The molecules in a lump of ice cling together firmly, but those in steam move so quickly that they escape completely from each other.

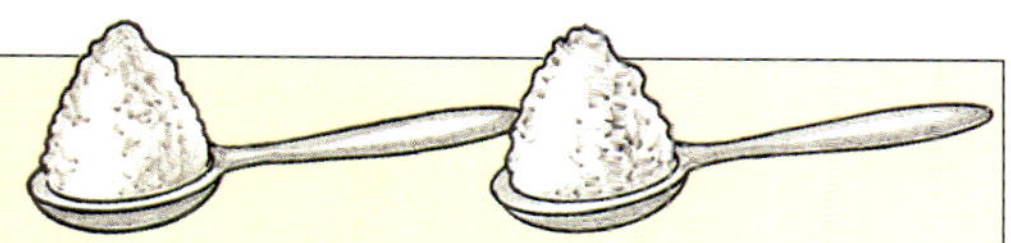

A single grain of sugar contains one million million million molecules of sugar. But the molecules in sugar and other solids, as well as in liquids and gases, are mostly empty space.

Imagine the molecules in a glass of water were made bigger so that they became the size of ping-pong balls. Each ball would be about 1 metre away from the next ball. In a cloud of steam, they would be over 1,000 metres from each other. Some water molecules in steam can travel as fast as Concorde – about 2,600 kilometres per hour.

3 After about 3-4 hours, the lollies will be solid. Remove the lollies from the moulds, and store them in a plastic container in the freezer.

Melting

An ice lolly is really a mixture of water and fruit juice which has been frozen into a solid. The molecules in a frozen ice lolly cling together firmly. They move backwards and forwards as they gently vibrate.

But when you eat an ice lolly in the hot sunshine, it soon starts to melt. A liquid drips from the lolly. Why does this happen, and what are the molecules doing now? The heat from the Sun makes the molecules inside the lolly vibrate more quickly. Soon they move so fast that they break away from each other. The solid ice lolly melts and turns into a liquid.

!

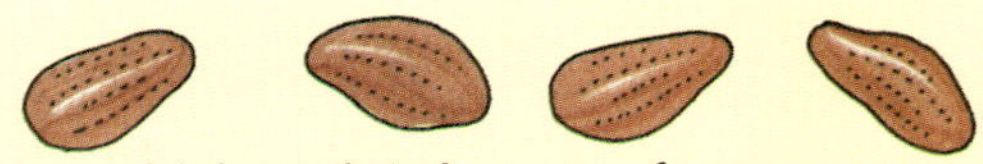

The word 'chocolate' comes from an Aztec word meaning 'cocoa water' or 'bitter water'. The Aztecs in Mexico made a chocolate drink by grinding cocoa beans, mixing them with water and spices, and heating the mixture to make a paste.

The paste was left to dry on leaves where it formed a solid block. The block was peeled off the leaf and mixed with hot water and maize to make a foaming hot chocolate drink.

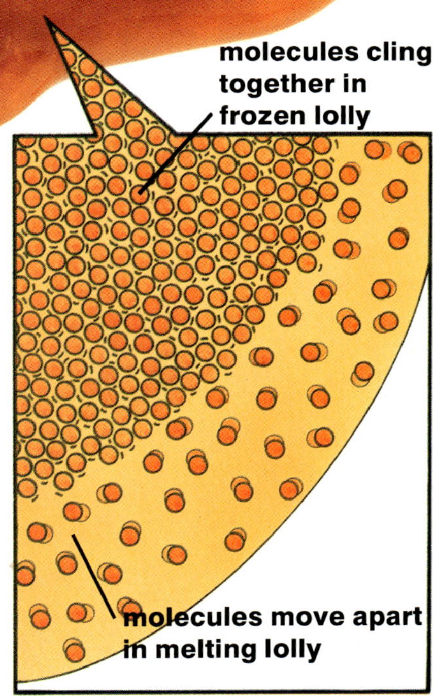

Other solids, like chocolate and butter, also melt when they are heated. The heat can come from hot sunshine or from a cooker, but the effect on the solid is the same. When liquid chocolate or butter cools, it turns back into a solid.

Chocolate treats

Ingredients
200g plain chocolate
small fruits, such as grapes, pineapple chunks, strawberries, cherries, raisins and dates

Equipment

a small glass jug or bowl
a saucepan
a wooden spoon
cocktail sticks
waxed paper

1 Break the chocolate into squares and put them into the jug or bowl. Ask an adult to help you boil about 5 cm of water in a pan. Turn down the heat.

2 Gently place the jug in the pan. Stir the chocolate until it melts. This takes about 3-5 minutes. Turn off the heat and take out the jug.

3 Push a cocktail stick into a piece of fruit and dip the fruit into the melted chocolate. Place it on the waxed paper until the chocolate hardens. Repeat with each fruit.

Disappearing water

A wet cloth dries out slowly when it's left out in the sun. When you boil an egg, the water level in the pan goes steadily down. The hotter the water becomes, the quicker it seems to disappear.

The molecules in a liquid move around freely, bumping into each other all the time. Sometimes a molecule travels very fast because it has been hit by other molecules all at the same time. Fast-moving molecules escape completely from the surface of the liquid.

As molecules escape, the liquid slowly evaporates and becomes a gas or vapour. But when water boils, so many molecules escape so quickly that vapour forms inside the liquid, and not just at its surface. Bubbles rise to the surface and burst, releasing vapour into the air. Water evaporates from fresh fruit that is put out to dry in the sunshine. This is how grapes become raisins, and plums become prunes.

!

The Tartars were a tribe of nomads who lived in Asia in the 13th century. They travelled long distances across the mountains, carrying all their food and drink supplies on horseback.

The Tartars dried the milk from their mares by leaving it in the sunshine. Water and dried milk were later placed in drinking bottles hung from the horsemen's saddles. The dried milk and water mixed to make liquid milk as the Tartars rode along.

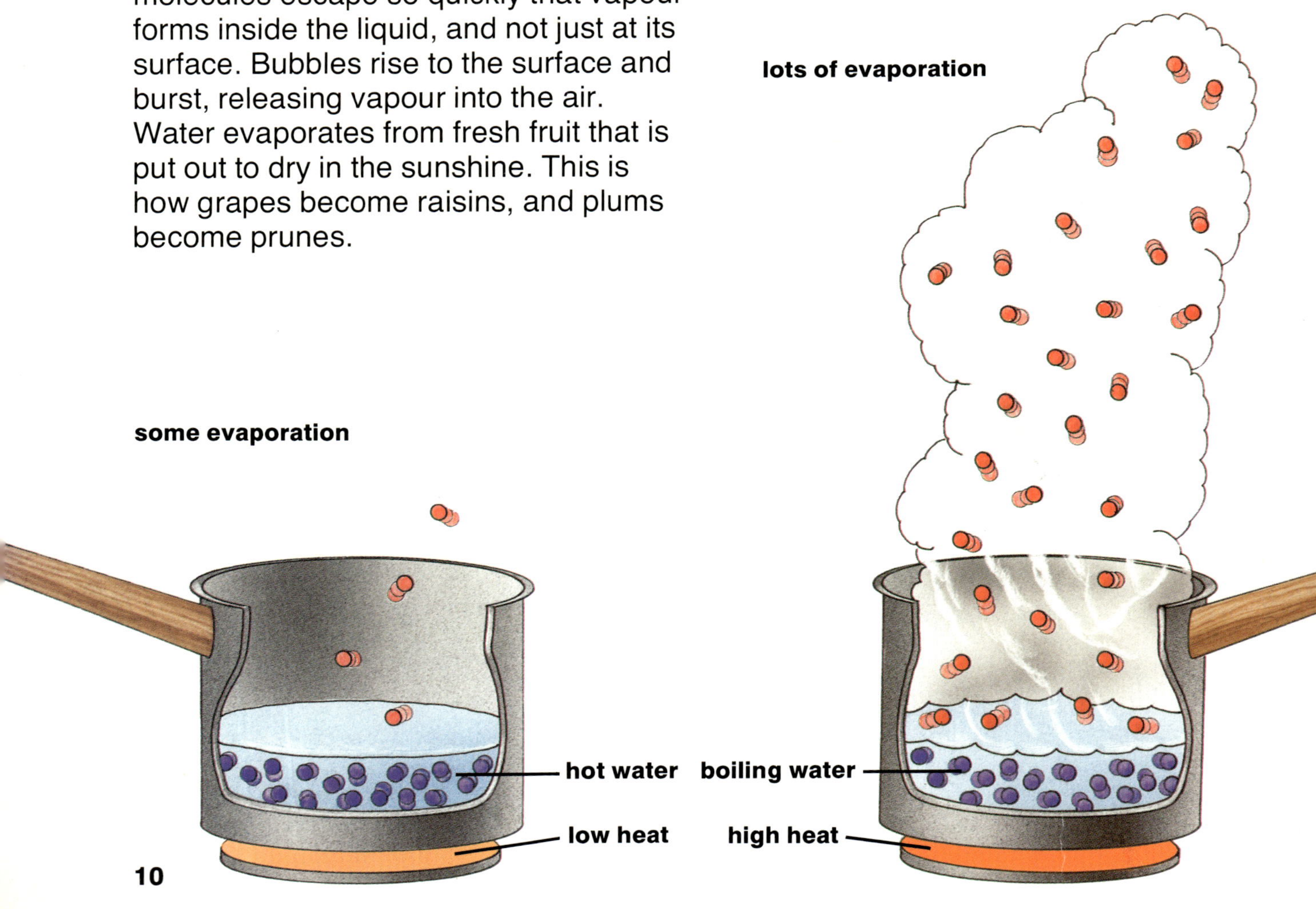

Tabbouleh

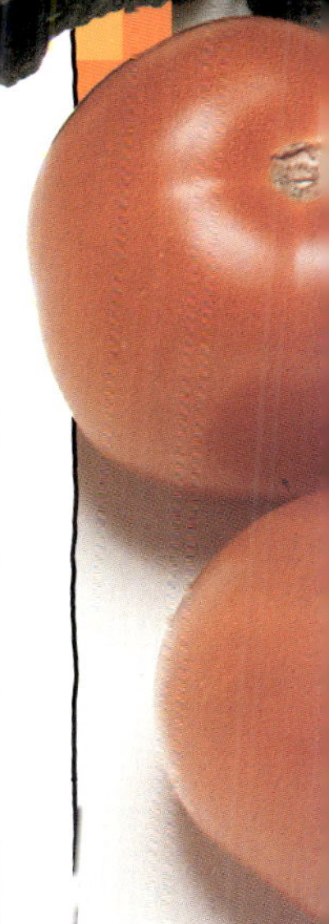

Ingredients

100g bulgar wheat
4 tablespoons fresh parsley
2 tablespoons fresh mint
2 tablespoons olive oil
6 spring onions
3 tomatoes
1 lemon
salt and pepper

Equipment

2 large bowls
a knife
a chopping board
a grater
a lemon squeezer
a sieve
a tablespoon

1 Put the bulgar wheat into a bowl and cover it with cold water. Leave it to soak for 20 minutes. The dried wheat swells as it soaks up water.

2 Grate the yellow skin of the lemon (not the white pith). Cut the lemon in half and squeeze out the juice. Put the rind and juice in the bowl.

3 Wash the parsley and mint, and chop finely. Wash the onions and remove the outer leaves. Chop the onions and tomatoes. Add the chopped ingredients to the bowl.

4 Drain the bulgar wheat and press out as much water as you can. Add it to the bowl, together with the oil, salt and pepper. Mix well and serve.

From a gas to a liquid

Drops of liquid water appear on the cold windows of a steamy kitchen. To find out where this water comes from, you must look back at the cooker.

Water evaporates and escapes from hot food and saucepans of boiling water. The air in the kitchen fills with water vapour, which is water in the form of a gas. The molecules in this gas are moving very fast, and the gas quickly spreads throughout the kitchen.

Some molecules hit the cold windows. They make the windows slightly warmer, and this cools the water vapour. The molecules in the cooled water vapour move more slowly now. They have less energy. They move closer and stick together in small groups. These groups join up to make the drops of water on the windows. So heat evaporates water to make water vapour. Cooled water vapour condenses to make liquid water.

When the warm air inside a room reaches the cold windows, the water vapour in the air cools and condenses to form drops of liquid water.

Steamed sponge pudding

Ingredients

2 tablespoons jam
2 eggs
2 tablespoons milk
175g self-raising flour
100g caster sugar
100g soft margarine

Equipment

weighing scales
a large saucepan with a lid, or a steamer
a pudding basin (900 ml size)
a tablespoon
a small bowl or jug
a fork
a mixing bowl
a wooden spoon
aluminium foil and string

1 Half fill the saucepan with water and ask an adult to help you boil the water.

2 Grease the pudding basin with a little margarine and put the jam into the bottom of it.

3 Break the eggs into the small bowl or jug. Add the milk and beat together well with a fork.

4 Put the flour, sugar and margarine into the large bowl. Add the egg and milk mixture and combine all the ingredients with a wooden spoon.

5 Pour the mixture over the jam in the basin. Cover the top of the basin with foil and tie a piece of string around it.

6 Ask an adult to stand the basin in the boiling water or the steamer. Put on the lid and steam for $1\frac{1}{2}$ hours. Add more water from time to time. Ask an adult to do this.

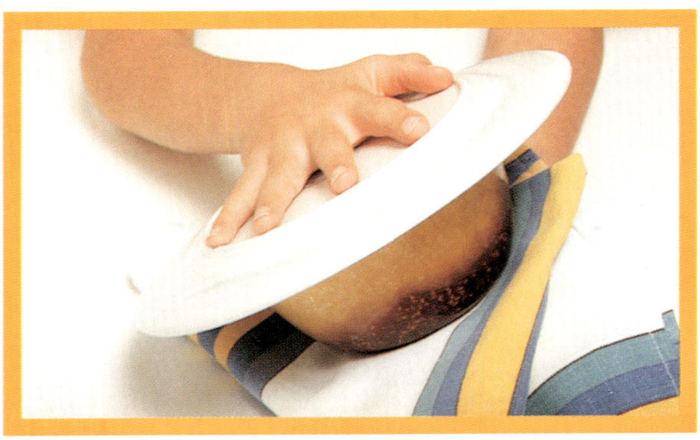

7 After $1\frac{1}{2}$ hours, carefully remove the basin from the pan or steamer. Take off the foil cover and turn the pudding out onto a plate.

What is temperature?

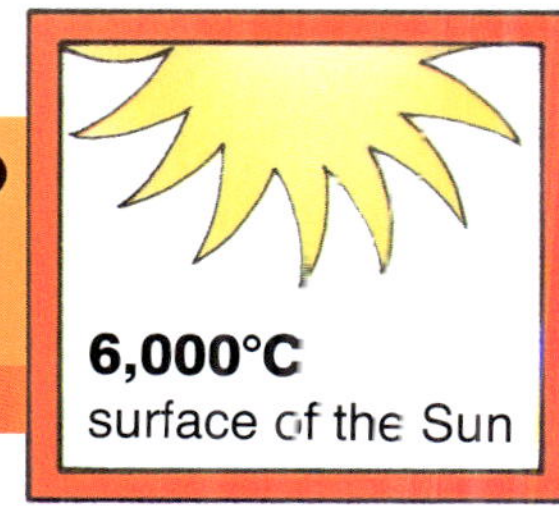

A recipe book tells you how hot your oven must be in order to cook different foods – very hot for baking biscuits, but cooler for cooking meringues. The oven's temperature tells you how hot it is. Temperature is measured in degrees Celsius, which is usually shortened to °C.

Ice melts at 0°C, water boils at 100°C and biscuits bake at about 200°C. The temperature of a freezer is between −10°C and −15°C. The freezer is between 10°C and 15°C colder than melting ice.

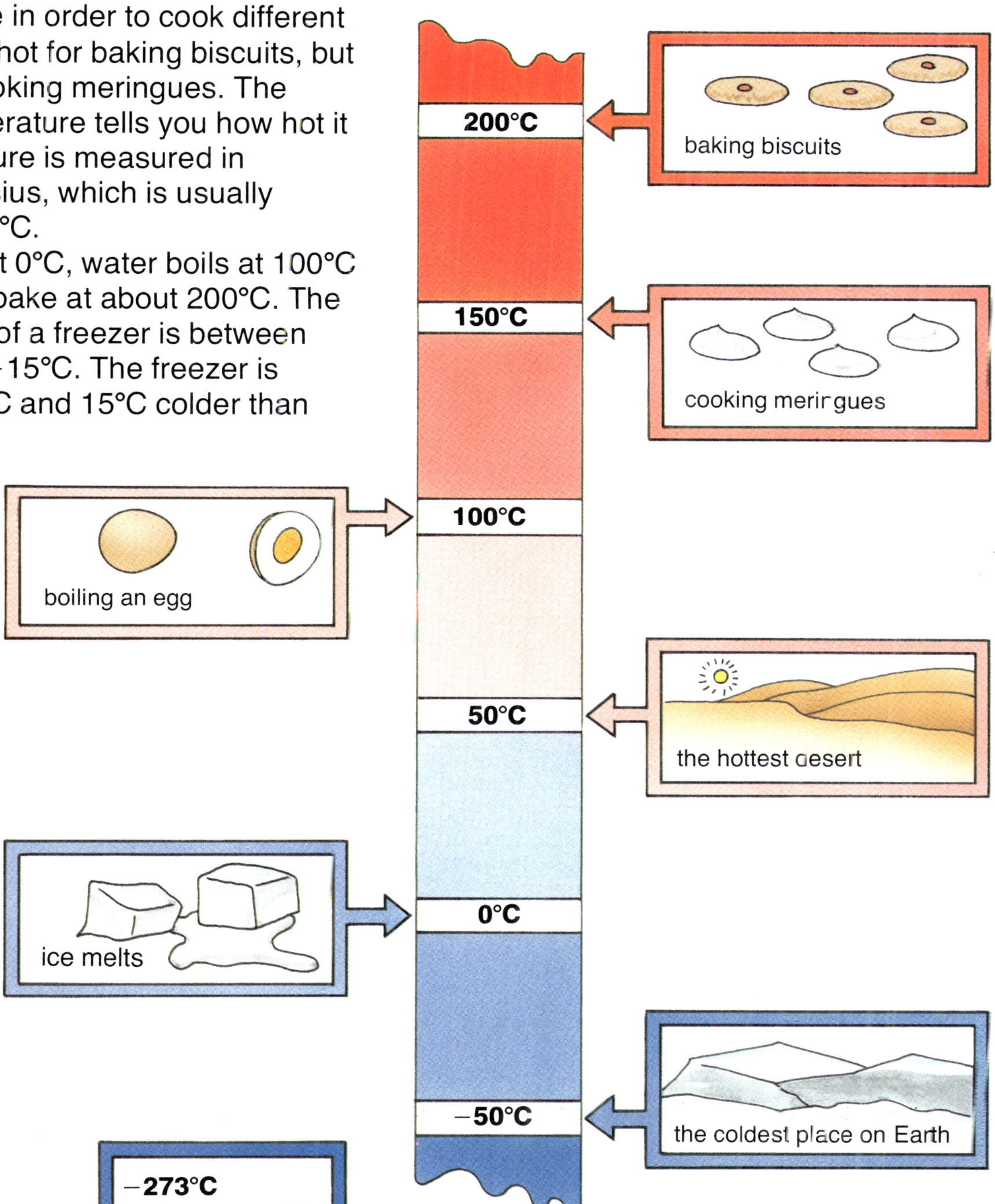

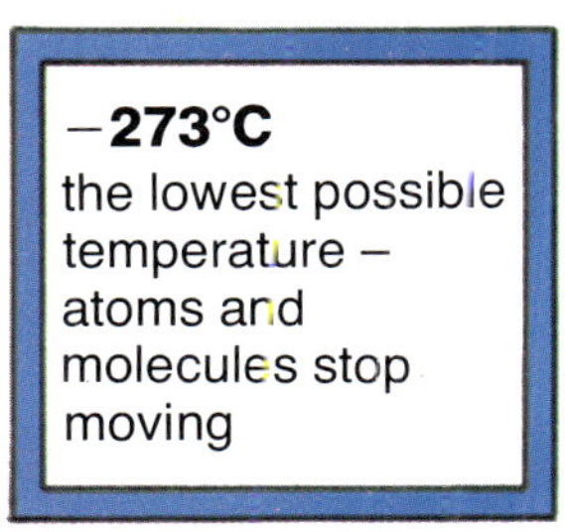

This diagram shows some temperatures marked on the Celsius scale, and some foods that cook at these temperatures.

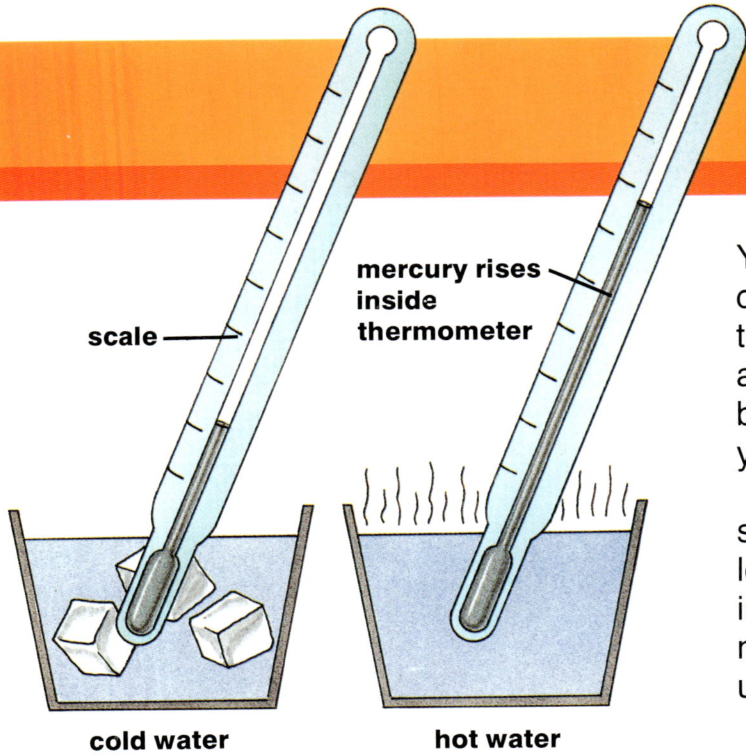

You use temperature to say how hot or cold things are. You measure temperature with a thermometer. There are many different sorts of thermometer, but most use the Celsius scale to tell you the temperature.

Glass thermometers contain a liquid, such as mercury or alcohol, inside a long, thin tube. The hotter the liquid inside the thermometer becomes, the more space it takes up. The liquid rises up inside the tube, which is marked with

Stuffed eggs

Ingredients

4 eggs
50g cottage cheese
1 tablespoon mayonnaise
salt and pepper
paprika

Equipment

a saucepan
a small bowl
a knife
a teaspoon
a tablespoon
a fork
a chopping board

1 Place the eggs in the saucepan and cover with cold water. Ask an adult to help you bring the water to the boil. Boil the eggs for 10 minutes.

2 When the eggs are cooked, switch off the heat and carefully drain off the hot water. Run cold water onto the eggs until they feel cold.

a temperature scale. Glass thermometers can accurately measure temperatures ranging from −50°C to 300°C. But they are fragile and break easily.

Cooking thermometers are tougher but they are not so accurate. They contain strips of metal that bend as they heat up. The bending metal moves a pointer on a scale. Digital thermometers are accurate but can be expensive.

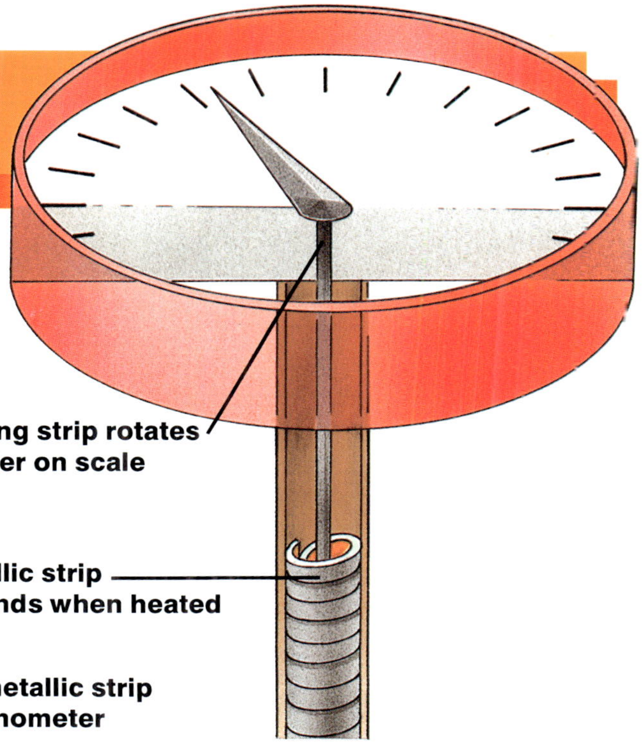

a bimetallic strip thermometer

3 Remove the shells and cut the eggs in half lengthways. Remove the yolks and use a fork to mash them in a bowl.

4 Add the cheese, mayonnaise, salt and pepper, and blend to a creamy mixture. Spoon the mixture into the egg halves and sprinkle with paprika.

Freezing cold

When you put fresh raspberries in the freezer, they become hard. The water inside the fruit freezes as it changes from a liquid to a solid. All the molecules in the raspberries slow down as the freezer takes away warmth from the fruit. The water molecules in the raspberries no longer move freely past each other. Instead, they join together in groups which make up crystals of ice.

Ice crystals take up more room than the liquid water that made them. Raspberries are made up from tiny bags called cells. Each cell has a thin wall. These walls burst when the water inside expands as the ice forms. So when you take frozen raspberries out of the freezer and leave them to thaw, they become limp and squashy. This is because all the cell walls are broken and so the liquid juices leak out.

!

The Romans made ice cream 2,000 years ago, but they didn't have freezers to help them. They used to make the liquid ice cream mixture in a small bowl. They placed the bowl in a larger bowl containing water, snow and ice from a frozen river.

Salt was then added to the water. As the salt dissolved in the water, the temperature of the water dropped by an extra 5°C or more. The ice cream mixture then froze into a solid.

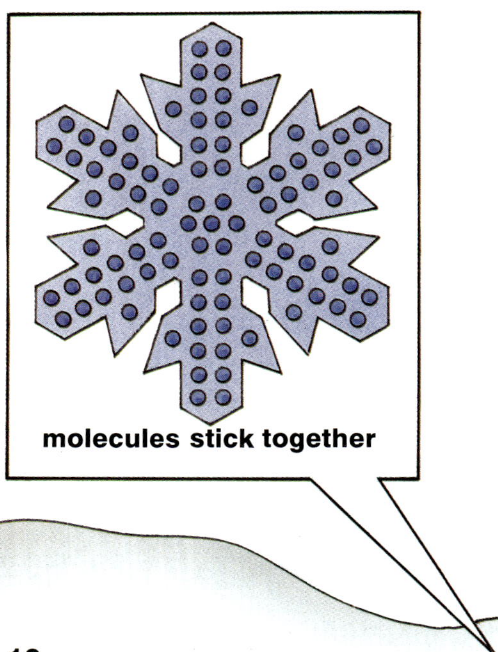

Banana and chocolate chip ice cream

Ingredients
300ml chilled double cream
50g caster sugar
1 banana
1 teaspoon vanilla essence
25g chocolate chips

Equipment
weighing scales
an electric or hand whisk
a bowl
a fork
a plate
a tablespoon
a flat container such as a baking tin
a plastic tub with a lid

1 Ask an adult to set the freezer or fridge to its coldest setting. Put the flat container in the freezer or ice box to chill.

2 Pour the cream into the bowl and whisk until it thickens. Peel the banana and mash it on the plate.

3 Add the banana, sugar, vanilla essence and chocolate chips to the cream. Mix gently until all the ingredients are combined.

4 Take the container out of the freezer and pour the mixture into it. Freeze it for about 1½ hours until it is just beginning to set solid.

5 Now transfer the ice cream mixture to the bowl. Beat with the whisk or a wooden spoon to break up the crystals of ice.

6 Spoon the mixture into the plastic tub with a lid. Place it in the freezer for 1 hour to complete the freezing process.

7 Take the ice cream out of the freezer 15 minutes before you want to eat it.

Getting bigger

A baked loaf of bread is much larger than the lump of wet dough that you put into the oven. When you cut into a loaf of bread, each slice seems to be full of tiny holes. Why do bread and cake mixtures get bigger as they cook?

Bakers add a substance called yeast when they are making dough, and cooks add a substance called baking powder to cake mixtures. Both yeast and baking powder give off tiny bubbles of gas when they are mixed with the flour and other ingredients. These bubbles are then trapped inside the mixtures. During baking, heat makes the gas expand and so the tiny bubbles swell. This makes the bread and cake mixtures rise.

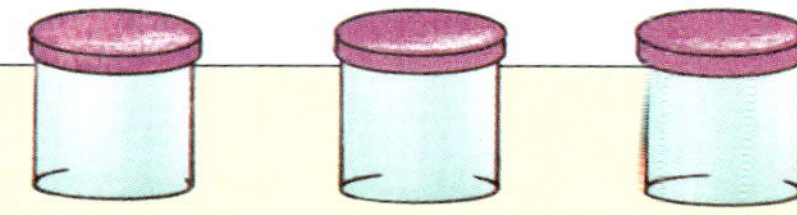

Have you ever found it difficult to open a jar of jam or honey? Some glass jars have very tight lids that are difficult to unscrew. If adults cannot unscrew a lid, they often hold the jar under a tap of hot running water. The metal lid becomes looser because it expands more than the glass jar.

Liquids expand when heated, but they also become more runny. Treacle and cooking oil are runny when hot, but sticky when they are cool.

freshly made dough **dough after it has risen** **baked bread**

Solids, liquids and gases all expand when heated. The atoms and molecules inside move faster. They push against each other more strongly and try to take up more room.

Before boiling an egg, you should first prick its blunt end with a pin. When the gas inside the egg expands during heating, it can escape through the tiny hole without cracking the eggshell.

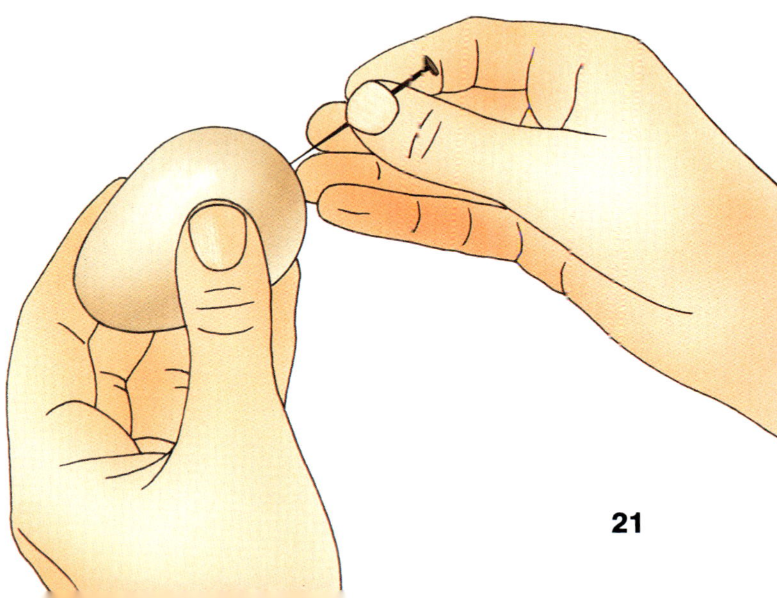

Wholemeal bread rolls

Ingredients

225g wholemeal flour
1 teaspoon salt
1 sachet 'easy-blend' or 'activated' dried yeast
190 ml warm water
a little vegetable oil

Equipment

a baking tray
weighing scales
a large bowl
a teaspoon
a measuring jug
a wooden spoon
a knife
a clean tea towel

1 Lightly grease the baking tray with a small amount of oil. Put the flour into the bowl and add the yeast and salt.

2 Mix the flour, yeast and salt thoroughly. Make a well in the middle of the mixture and pour in the warm water.

3 Mix in the water with the wooden spoon. When it is too hard to stir with the spoon, use your hands. The mixture will form a clump of dough.

4 Sprinkle some flour onto a work surface. Knead the dough with your fists for 3–4 minutes. If the dough is sticky, sprinkle on more flour.

5 Use the knife to divide the dough into 6 equal pieces. Knead each piece, then shape it into a ball and place on the oiled baking tray.

6 Wet the tea towel and wring it out well until it is just damp. Place it over the rolls and put them in a warm place for about 1 hour.

7 Ask an adult to help you pre-heat the oven to 200°C. When the rolls have risen, bake them in the oven for 15 minutes. Leave the rolls to cool for a few minutes before eating.

Heat on the move

A saucepan full of boiling water is dangerously hot, but the pan's handle is cool enough to hold. Saucepans are made from metals like aluminium, copper and stainless steel. Metals are good conductors of heat. This means that heat from the cooker passes easily into the saucepan. The handle is made from plastic or wood, which are not good conductors of heat. Plastic, wood and many other solids are insulators. This means that heat does not easily pass through them.

Liquids are poor conductors of heat. Most foods contain a lot of water. If you grill a sausage too quickly, the outside will burn while the inside is still raw. Food cooks as the water slowly conducts heat from the outside to the inside. Gases are insulators, too. A picnic cool box is lined with plastic foam. Gas trapped in the foam conducts heat into the box very slowly, so the food inside will stay cool for a long time.

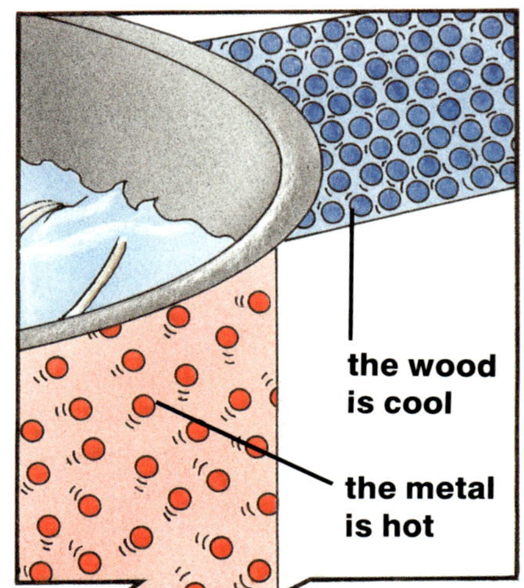

Expensive cups and saucers are usually made from a type of china called porcelain. It is very hard and strong, and it is also an insulator.

Porcelain is made from a special clay and was invented by the Chinese in the 1st century AD. It came to Europe about 350 years ago, when traders in sailing ships started to bring tea from China. Tea is best drunk when hot, and so the traders brought porcelain cups from China as well. Drinks stay hot in porcelain cups.

Chinese stir fry

Ingredients

4 spring onions
1 red pepper
2 celery sticks
50g mushrooms
2 teaspoons cornflour
150 ml water
2 tablespoons soy sauce
1 tablespoon tomato puree
1 tablespoon vegetable oil
100g shelled prawns

Equipment

a chopping board
a wok or large frying pan
a knife
a tablespoon
a wooden spoon
a measuring jug
a teaspoon

1 Wash the vegetables. Take the core and seeds out of the pepper. Ask an adult to help you cut the vegetables into 'sticks' of the same size.

2 Put the cornflour into the jug and add water to the 150-ml mark. Stir well, then add the soy sauce and tomato puree. Stir again to blend.

3 Ask an adult to help you heat the oil in the wok or pan. Cook the onion, pepper and celery for 3 minutes on a high heat, stirring with the wooden spoon.

4 Add the prawns and mushrooms and stir fry for 3 minutes. Add the mixture in the jug to the pan (it will sizzle). Keep stirring until bubbling and hot. Serve at once.

What is convected heat?

The top shelf inside a gas oven is hotter than the shelves lower down. Burning gas heats the air at the bottom of the oven. The hot air expands, takes up more space and rises to the top of the oven. When heat travels with a moving gas or liquid, the movement is called convection.

Convection carries heat through water to the food cooking in a saucepan. The water at the bottom of the pan becomes hotter. It rises upwards, cools and then sinks slowly downwards. As the water moves, it becomes hot all the way through. These movements in heated liquids and gases are called convection currents. They move quite slowly.

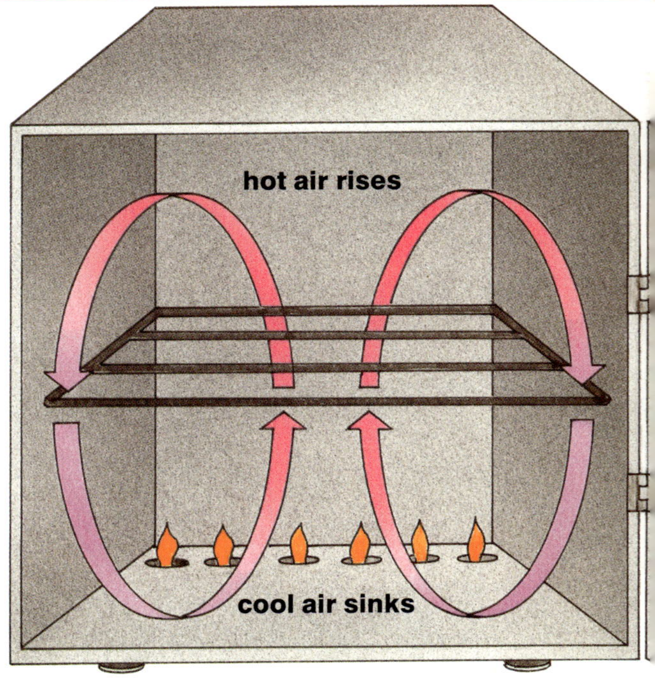

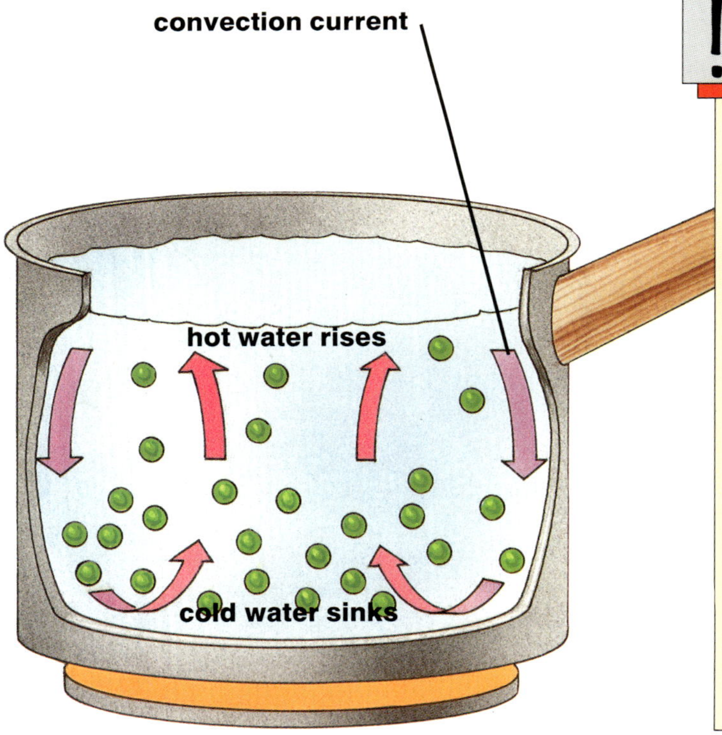

!

Centuries ago, the Maori people in New Zealand did not make pottery, and so they had no leakproof pots or containers in which to boil water over a fire. Instead, they filled a wooden bowl with cold water and placed the food to be cooked in the water. Then they dropped a hot stone to the bottom of the bowl.

The heat from the stone was carried by convection currents up through the water to the food.

Sea shell salad

Ingredients

100g pasta shells
1 red pepper
1 small onion
a small tin of sweetcorn
2 tablespoons mayonnaise
1 tablespoon natural yoghurt
salt and pepper
fresh parsley

Equipment

a saucepan
a colander
a chopping board
a knife
a tin opener
a sieve
a large bowl
a small bowl
a fork
a tablespoon
a serving bowl

1 Ask an adult to help you boil a pan of water. When the water is boiling, add the pasta and boil for 10–12 minutes. Do not cover with a lid.

2 Drain the cooked pasta through the colander and run cold water over it until cool. Leave the pasta to drain.

3 Wash the pepper and remove the core and seeds. Chop the pepper and onion into small pieces and place in the large bowl.

4 Carefully open the tin of sweetcorn and drain through the sieve. Throw away the liquid and add the drained sweetcorn to the bowl.

5 Add the pasta to the bowl and mix all the ingredients together with a spoon.

6 Put the mayonnaise and yoghurt in the small bowl. Add the salt and pepper and stir well. Pour the mayonnaise mixture over the salad.

7 Mix the salad gently so that the dressing covers all the ingredients. Put into the serving bowl and sprinkle with chopped parsley.

What is radiant heat?

Food cooks quickly when you place it under a hot grill. But how does the heat move downwards from the grill to the food? It cannot move by convection, which only carries heat upwards. It cannot move by conduction, because the air between the grill and the food is an insulator and so it doesn't carry heat well. A grill depends on radiant heat to cook the food. Radiant heat travels in straight lines and as fast as light. The sunlight that warms the Earth is also radiant heat.

radiant heat cooks the food in a grill

radiant heat travels from the Sun to the Earth in straight lines

!

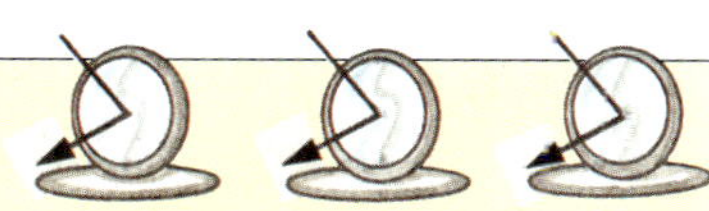

People who live in sunny countries can use sunlight to cook their food outdoors. They use mirrors to catch the radiant heat from the Sun. This heat is then directed onto a black metal box that contains the food. Black is the best colour for taking in, or absorbing, the radiant heat. The Sun's heat then cooks the food inside the box.

Further things to do

Wrap squares of chocolate in pieces of aluminium foil and put them in a bowl of hot water. When the water is cold (after about 3 hours), unwrap the chocolate. Can you explain its new shape?

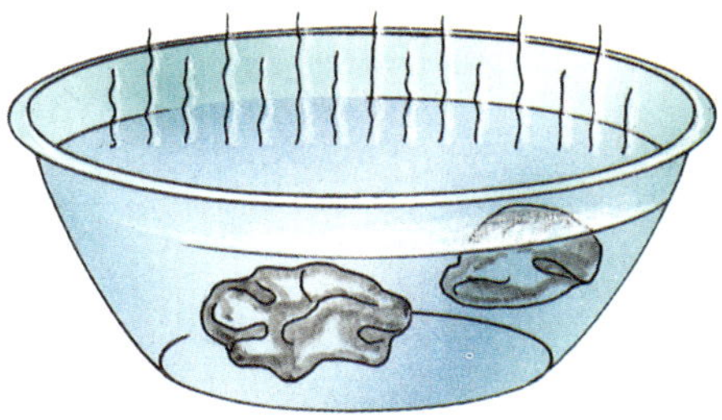

Place a small plum and a grape on a baking tray and stand it on a hot radiator for a few days. The result should be a prune and a raisin.

Hold a plastic teaspoon (an insulator) in one hand and a metal teaspoon (a conductor) in the other. Dip both spoons at the same time into a cup of hot tea. Wait for a few moments, and then explain what each spoon feels like.

Take two glass tumblers and place one inside the fridge. After 30 minutes, put both tumblers side by side on a table. Breathe into each one. The cold glass becomes cloudier more quickly. The water vapour in your breath condenses more easily on the cold glass.

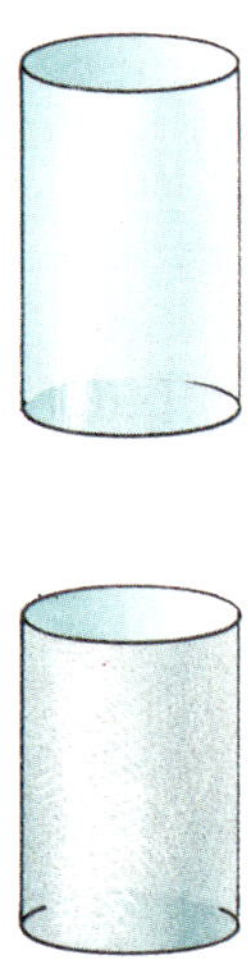

Fill a heat-resistant glass saucepan with cold water. Place it on the cooker for 5 minutes, without any heat, until the water stops moving. Drop a hard-boiled brightly coloured fruit sweet into the water and warm the pan gently. As the sweet dissolves, streams of colour appear in the water. They show the movement of the water as convection currents carry the heat through it.

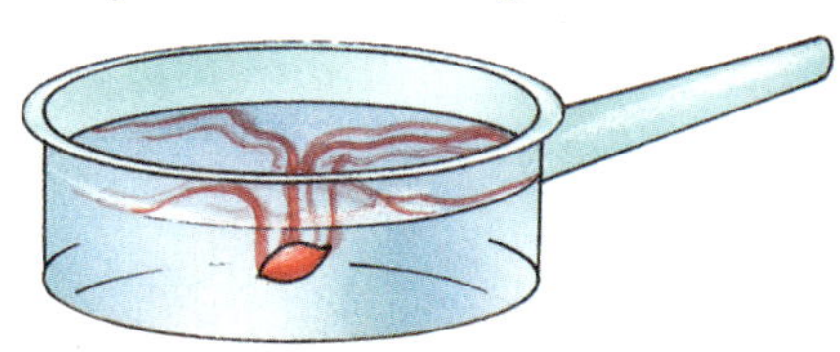

Glossary

atom
The smallest part of any substance. All solids, liquids and gases are made up from atoms.

baking powder
A white powder that gives off a gas when mixed with water. The gas makes cakes rise during cooking.

boil
A change that happens to a very hot liquid. Bubbles of gas quickly grow in the liquid, rise to the surface and burst.

condense
A change that happens to a gas or vapour when it is cooled. The result is a liquid.

conduction
The way in which heat travels through a solid from a hot part to a cooler part.

conductor
A substance that allows heat to flow easily through it. The substance stays still while the heat flows.

convection
The way in which liquids or gases move as they carry heat from a warm place to a cooler place.

convection current
The movement of a stream of hot gas or liquid that happens during convection.

crystal
A small piece of solid with straight sides. All the crystals in a substance have the same shape.

degree Celsius
A unit that is used to measure temperature. It is written as °C for short. Many thermometers have a scale marked in degrees Celsius.

evaporate
The way in which a liquid slowly changes into a gas or vapour.

expand
To get bigger. Solids, liquids and gases expand when they are heated.

freeze
The way in which a liquid changes into a solid when it is cooled.

gas
A substance, such as air, that is neither a solid nor a liquid. A gas will escape unless it is kept in a closed container.

insulator
A substance that does not allow heat to flow through it.

liquid
A substance that is runny and is neither a solid nor a gas. A liquid stays in the bottom of its container.

melt
The way in which a solid changes into a liquid when it is heated.

molecule
A tiny part that makes up most substances. All the molecules in a substance are the same. Each molecule contains two or more atoms.

radiant heat
A kind of heat that travels in a straight line across empty spaces.

scale
A row of marks with numbers that is used to measure something.

solid
A substance that keeps its shape. Unlike a liquid or a gas, a solid does not flow.

temperature
A kind of measurement that shows how hot or cold something is. Thermometers measure temperature, usually in degrees Celsius.

vapour
The gas that is given off by all liquids, even when they are not hot enough to boil.

yeast
A simple kind of fungus that helps dough to rise. Yeast can be used either fresh or dried.

Index